The 1913 Solution

How the 17ᵗʰ Amendment is Destroying

the United States of America

HR Stuart

The 1913 Solution

How the 17th Amendment is Destroying

the United States of America

Written by HR Stuart

Printed by CreateSpace, An Amazon.com Company

2016

Dedication

To My Dutch Girl

Contents

Introduction

Do you believe

- The federal government is too big & too powerful?
- Balanced budgets are important or that $20 trillion is too much debt?
- Our federal government is taxing too much?
- Our federal government is enacting too many regulations?
- Laws should apply to the "ruling class" and not just to common citizens?
- We are losing our freedom?
- In term limits?
- In Campaign Finance Reform?
- The mainstream media is too powerful?
- Political correctness has been used as a weapon to silence opposing views?
- Politicians are intentionally dividing us into groups and then driving a wedge between these groups?
- Our values & our culture are being compromised – or discarded?
- Our nation's future looks bleak?

If you answered "yes" to any of these questions, this book is for you. It contains a relatively simple solution to many of the issues we face today. We can restore our nation to greatness and secure our long-term viability and prosperity without relying on the politicians or bureaucrats in Washington, D.C.

What Happened?

A relatively simple solution is available to us that will effectively address many of the problems we currently face as a nation. To understand this solution, we need to understand our history and how we went astray with the grand experiment we know and love as the United States of America.

Prior to 1913, the United States generally conformed to the provisions of the Constitution. The federal government was constrained and controlled by the people and the several states. Each level of government was (more or less) appropriately sized, power was divided between local, state and federal levels and further separated between the three branches at the federal level. Back then, the federal government worked for us.

Today, we work for the federal government. Those of us remaining in the workforce have to work the first third of each year just to pay our federal income taxes and this doesn't even consider the myriad of federal excise taxes (e.g., on fuel) or other surcharges. This is an excessive burden that discourages hard work, risk and entrepreneurialism.

The burden doesn't just fall on individuals either. Federal regulations mandate onerous requirements and restrictions on the operation of our businesses reducing profitability. According to the

Small Business Administration[1], approximately half of new businesses fail by the end of the fourth year. Not surprisingly, many of the leading causes of business failures are related to finances in one way or another. When the federal government regulates and taxes businesses at high levels, it establishes a difficult environment in which to start and operate a successful business. As we look back over the last hundred years, the increasing burden of the federal government is driving an increased emphasis on efficiency and we see fewer examples of craftsmanship.

Even established businesses are reluctant to hire new employees given the associated costs of employment and regulatory compliance. The number of able-bodied workers without jobs now exceeds 90 million. In a nation of 320 million people (which includes children and the elderly), 90 million unemployed ought to raise serious public policy questions.

Beyond the regulatory and taxation environment, there are many other signs that we've lost control of the federal government. The executive branch refuses to enforce the laws duly passed by the legislative branch and signed into law. In other cases, the president has approved requests for exceptions to a law. A president assumes dictatorial power when he decides what laws to enforce and which to ignore. Presidents have also assumed dictatorial power by use of executive orders that completely circumvent the legislative process. This is inconsistent with our Constitution-based government, yet the legislative and judicial branches choose not to take action.

The legislative branch, even when controlled by the political opposition, act as if they are powerless to stop or even slow the destructive initiatives and policies advanced by the president (or executive branch). One begins to wonder if these legislators have any interest in blocking un-constitutional initiatives that will grow the federal government. Many legislators may like a growing federal

---

[1] www.sba.gov/sites/default/files/FAQ_March_2014_0.pdf

government since in the long-run, it confers additional power and prestige to themselves. The president and each legislator swears an oath of office to defend the Constitution, yet this oath seems to have lost all meaning. This attitude has also crept into the judicial branch.

The Supreme Court consistently rules as if they have no understanding of the Constitution and some wonder how many of the justices have even read the document. A majority of the justices now feel free to interpret the Constitution in any way they please so as to advance their political agenda. They redefine terms and parse the various clauses of the Constitution while ignoring the overall premise of the document.

So what exactly did happen?

The 1913 Solution

1913 was a watershed year for the United States of America. A brief comparison of American history before and after 1913 using any number of criteria will demonstrate this assertion. The most dramatic and obvious change is in the rate of growth of the U.S. federal government. The federal government has grown in many ways;

- The number of federal workers
- The number of regulations
- The number of federal departments, agencies and programs
- The amount of federal government tax revenue from taxpayers and businesses
- The amount of federal government spending

These growth metrics are impressive even when viewed on a per capita basis. One important growth metric is federal spending as a percentage of Gross Domestic Product (GDP) or Gross National Product (GNP). According to the federal government's Historical Tables[2] printed with the 2013 Budget, as late as 1930, the federal

---

[2] Table 1.2 – Summary of Receipts, Outlays and Surpluses or Deficits as Percentages of GDP: 1930-2017, Fiscal Year 2013 Historical Tables; Budget of the U.S. Government, Office of Management and Budget

government spent 3.4% of the GNP. By 2009, the federal government spent over 24% of GDP.

Despite the claims of some politicians, money extracted from the private sector for government programs does not help to grow our economy. Because of the specter of profit (and loss) the private sector is better positioned to direct the use of these funds in the most productive manner. Extraction of nearly one-fourth of our economy each year is an enormous overhead burden on our businesses and everyone who works hard to make a productive contribution to our society especially in a modern age of global competition. If you've wondered why it is cheaper or more cost-effective to outsource manufacturing & industrial production to other countries, look no further than the U.S. federal government and the overhead costs it imposes on U.S. businesses. This increasing overhead burden is another manifestation of the growth in power and scope of the federal government.

> *Federal government spending as a percentage of our GDP has increased nearly tenfold since 1913.*

The federal government naturally grew from three major legislative changes enacted in 1913; the 16th and 17th Amendments to the U.S. Constitution and the Federal Reserve Act. These three changes comprise "The 1913 Solution".

The 1913 Solution transformed our national government from a relatively small, well-constrained servant of the states and the people to the bureaucratic behemoth (i.e., leviathan) we now see. These three legislative changes are the root cause of many of the challenges we face today. They each contributed to a fundamental transformation of our federal government, our nation and our prospects for the future.

16th Amendment

The first leg of the 1913 Solution was the 16th Amendment. The 16th Amendment was ratified in February of 1913. With the 16th

Amendment, the federal government formally established the power to impose direct taxes on the income of individual citizens, the power to determine how much and what types of income to tax and the power associated with directing how this money is to be spent. With a stroke of a pen, we the people became subservient to the federal government; no longer are we free or sovereign individuals protected by our federal government.

Many have expressed that a government big enough to give you everything you want is powerful enough to take everything you have. While this axiom resonates with some, others find it useless. Some argue that a government of virtually any size has sufficient power to take all you have. They may be missing the point. Here, we aren't necessarily considering the size or capabilities of the police state relative to our personal defense system, but the legal or lawful authority to take your property. With the 16th Amendment ratified, the government established the "legal" grounds to take as much of your income as they please.

17th Amendment

In April of 1913, just three short months after the ratification of the 16th Amendment, the 17th Amendment was ratified changing the selection process for United States senators. Under the original structure, our founding fathers specified that senators would be appointed by the legislatures of the states. In the pre-1913 era, senators were special envoys from the states to the federal government. These envoys represented state interests in Washington, D.C. – not necessarily the interests of the citizens of the states, but state

> *Our founding fathers intended senators to be special envoys from the state legislatures to the federal government to represent the interests of state governments at the federal level.*

interests from each state legislature's perspective. With the 17ᵗʰ Amendment, we now popularly elect our senators.

Hardly anyone talks about the 17ᵗʰ Amendment and while it doesn't seem like a major change, it may be the most significant change that has ever been made to the Constitution. It fundamentally altered the power structure of the federal government by weakening the checks and balances established by our founding fathers.

The 17ᵗʰ Amendment severed the formal oversight of the federal government by the states. In a very real sense, the 17ᵗʰ Amendment eliminated our adult supervision of the federal government.

As a result of the 17ᵗʰ Amendment, the Senate is no longer fulfilling its original Constitutional charter. It is no longer the voice of state interests in Washington. Worse, it is a super-House with little accountability making it essentially free to advance the personal interests of each senator.

The 17th Amendment may be the most deplorable change ever made to our Constitution. For those who could see the potential and supported the ratification of the 17ᵗʰ, it was diabolical in both scope and in subtlety.

Federal Reserve Act

The third leg of the 1913 Solution was the Federal Reserve Act. When this act passed in December of 1913, it established a new credit and monetary system controlled by central bankers. In a practical sense, this act removed the USA from a gold standard since the Federal Reserve was authorized to create money (or credit) from nothing. The currency created by the Federal Reserve is not backed by gold at Fort Knox or by anything tangible. Many worry about how much money has been created and whether our nation could survive a crisis resulting from an overabundance of un-backed (or fiat) currency. Some might argue that the Federal Reserve has helped to finance our nation's prosperity over the last hundred years, but it, along with the other provisions of the 1913 Solution, may have established the systemic problems that will lead to the ultimate demise of the United States of America.

United States of America 2.0

The 1913 Solution essentially established a new federal government; call it U.S. Government 2.0. It was a federal government no longer constrained by a lack of fiscal leverage and no longer governed by state interests. Mix in a hundred years of presidential visionaries as well as unrestrained legislative and judicial creativity (and constant prodding by special interests) and we now have a federal government no longer limited to the provisions of the Constitution.

We the People (or our founding fathers on our behalf) wrote the U.S. Constitution to protect our interests from an overbearing federal government. These men took great care in formulating the Constitution so as to limit the authority of those who would serve us from within the federal government. Many of our founding fathers were afraid of another King lording over us. Our founding fathers insisted the Constitution must constrain the power and authority of the federal government.

The 1913 Solution compromised these original provisions and opened the door to the leviathan of a federal government that we have today.

We the people now face a decision. We need to either commit ourselves to work harder and harder to cope with a federal government which is likely to become a heavier and heavier burden until the entire system collapses or we must find a way to regain control over it. Right now, no one is safe from the vagaries of the ruling class. Worse, our current trajectory essentially guarantees the ultimate demise of the United States of America either due to catastrophic financial collapse, chaotic internal strife, via takeover or destruction by another group of people. The signs are already apparent.

Time is short. With $19 trillion of debt (or probably much more), we have enslaved ourselves and our children for the foreseeable future.

We are living beyond our means and spending the earnings of future generations. And for what? Many of them will never enjoy the benefit of our excess. In reality, many of those employed (and productive) today are not enjoying the benefits of this excess either. The only real winners in the current system are the politicians, the bureaucrats and the special interest organizations in Washington, D.C. – i.e., the "Establishment".

With a federal government determined to control and mandate virtually every aspect of our lives, political power grows while our freedom diminishes.

Fortunately, our nation has a history that includes the keys to success. Fortunately, we can reverse the course of our nation and restore its future for our children and grandchildren. The USA has the culture and the Constitution established to be one of the freest nations on earth. Nowhere else will you find a better foundation for a great nation. The fight for the continued existence of the USA is a fight worth waging. It may not be too late, but time is short.

The Devilish Details...

Systemic Alterations

The first step to restore the USA is the repeal of the 17th Amendment. This may seem like an odd place to begin especially given the magnitude of our problems today, however the 17th Amendment may be the most significant change ever made to our Constitution. The 17th altered our entire structure of representative government from the states to the federal government.

While the 16th Amendment and the Federal Reserve Act provided the financial power to grow the size and scope of the federal government, the 17th Amendment provided the political structure (and power) to do so. There may be sufficient justification for a repeal of the 16th Amendment or a dismantling of the Federal Reserve, but the emphasis of this pamphlet is exploring the negative ramifications of (and the rationale to repeal) the 17th Amendment.

The 17th Amendment has had many negative ramifications. Many people probably don't know to attribute these symptoms to the 17th Amendment. One of the primary purposes of this booklet is to identify these ramifications and make the important connections between them and the 17th Amendment, i.e., connecting the symptoms to the root cause. A correct diagnosis is essential for fixing the systemic problems we now face.

Senators

The first symptom or negative ramification we'll consider is the extreme politicization of senators. Prior to 1913, to be appointed, a candidate for the U.S. Senate would need to garner the support of a majority of the members of the state legislature. This would typically require a bona fide statesman or diplomat; someone who appealed to both sides of the political aisle. Stridently advancing a political agenda that did not advance state or national interests would not likely garner a sufficient level of support within the state legislature to secure the appointment.

Once appointed, a senator would have been expected to faithfully represent the state's interests at the federal level. Members of the state legislature would have been astute watchdogs ever vigilant of their senators' activities and votes. This is in direct contrast to the senatorial politics we see today.

The 17th Amendment severed the relationship between senators and their state's government opening the door to the influence of special interests.

Today we see senators "playing" politics with every issue. Rather than being statesmen (or cooling the legislative process), senators now lead the political fights. Senators are political to the point of making ridiculous assertions to advance an ideology or legislative initiative.

The behavior of our senators has changed, but so has the nature of their service to their home states.

Vacuum Formed

Aristotle is credited with the quote, "Nature abhors a vacuum." He was actually referring to physics, but many systems exhibit this behavior. The 17th Amendment formed a political vacuum of sorts. Senators no longer saw the need to represent the interests of their state

15

legislature since there was no longer any accountability to these legislators.

The new constituencies, the registered voters of each state, did not and probably could not stay sufficiently informed. In 1913, information was slow and limited at best. Television and computers were not available. Radio was in its infancy. According to one source, the first radio news program didn't air until 1920. Newspapers were the only source of information for the first several years after 1913, so senators were suddenly free to advance whatever interests they believed they could politically justify and often, little justification was needed.

The political vacuum formed by the 17th Amendment was quickly and effectively filled by what is commonly referred to as "special interests".

The 17th Amendment unshackled senators. Even with the advent of radio, television and the internet, senators are free to advance whatever special interest they want with little risk of a serious challenge to their seat. Most voters don't take the time to educate themselves and are not well-informed – although many of these "low information voters" believe themselves to be well-informed. In reality, all of us suffer from a level of situational ignorance. We can't possibly know all the inner workings of Congress or the federal government.

Aside from the limitations associated with not having a direct pipeline of information from Congressional inner chambers, most people are too busy to carefully read the bills voted on by the Senate or to track the voting records of their senators over each six-year term. Most legislation is titled something very favorable that is hard to oppose like "The Affordable Care Act" and some of these bills contain thousands of pages of convoluted provisions, so unless they take the time to read and study the bill, most voters are not likely to understand the negative implications or unintended consequences just from the title of the bill.

By the way, the complexity and length of proposed legislation doesn't just deter the voting public. Many senators don't bother to read the text of each bill in its entirety prior to casting their vote either.

The 17th Amendment even changed the inherent standard for new legislation. Originally, for a bill to become law, it had to be in the interest of a majority of the people and in the interest of a majority of the states – or at least a majority of the representatives of each. This is a high standard. Since the 17th Amendment, a bill needs to simply pass a series of votes by popularly elected representatives under the heavy influence of the national media. This is a much different standard, as well as a different mode of operation and it leads to a number of negative implications just from this one aspect of the 17th.

Even though senators are popularly elected, they not only don't advance the interests of the state, they often don't advance the interests of the people who elected them either. Often, senators advance special interests to the detriment of their states' interests or the general interests of the people.

Special Interests

There are countless organizations that lobby to advance special interests. Special interest organizations have become big business in and around the Washington, D.C. area since 1913. Many of these organizations advance interests that promote a very specific industry or a cause.

The genesis of new legislation or regulation is often the identification of an issue by one of these special interest organizations. Typically, success for one interest is to the detriment of another. In many cases, it is not clear that the laws passed, the programs funded, or the regulations enacted advance our national interests or the interests of any state.

Prior to 1913, Washington lobbyists would have had a much more difficult challenge since senators would have been much less likely to advance a special interest that did not also advance the interests of their state (from the state legislature's perspective) or our long-term national interests. Attempting to convince the senators from 25 or more states that a bill is in our national interest or in the interests of each of their states would be a more difficult task than convincing a few leaders of a political party who might be looking for a generous financial contribution.

Professor Eugene C. Brooks wrote a book in 1916 called "Woodrow Wilson as President". Brooks was a Professor of Education at Trinity College. This book is of particular interest in preparing this pamphlet since it was written and published during Wilson's first term in office. It provides an interesting perspective of the national mood and of President Wilson's mindset through the eyes of a 'higher-information voter' living at the time. In the following passage, President Wilson and a senator are decrying the very notion that a lobbyist could be involved in the legislative process:

> ".... If the lobbyists were planning at that time a great attack on the bill, the President so timed his remarks as to create consternation among them, and then he was accused of using all the privilege and authority of his party leadership in order to rush 'an important piece of legislation through Congress.' The Senate at once asked for an investigation. Mr. Wilson said he could furnish names of leading lobbyists. 'A lobby in Washington; the idea!' And they ridiculed the President and even called him a lobbyist."

This passage supports the assertion that up until 1913 (and even into 1916 when the book was published), the very thought of lobbyists in Washington, D.C. was novel; a new and strange notion or at least not the ordinary state of affairs from the Senate's perspective (or at least this is what the senator(s) wanted the public to believe). Today, there is no doubt and no attempt to hide the fact that the lobbying industry in Washington, D.C. is big business.

Political Parties

Though it may seem a bit odd to think of a political party as a special interest, the major political parties are among the largest and most powerful special interest organizations. Most senators ardently adhere to and advance the interests of their political party often to the detriment of state and national interests.

Generally, senators vote based on the wishes of their political party leadership (regardless of the consensus of their state legislators). The political party helped to get them elected, so there is inevitably some allegiance formed or favors owed. This is a natural result of the relationships forged over the last hundred years and highlights one of the most egregious aspects of the systemic problems created by the 17th Amendment.

Access & Influence

Aside from the formally organized special interests, there are times when an individual citizen attempts to influence a senator. In this regard, the individual citizen may be the smallest and least powerful special interest. Prior to 1913, it would have been the exception for an individual citizen to contact and attempt to influence a U.S. senator. Why would they? Senators answered to their state legislature.

With the 17th Amendment, the individual citizen becomes one of the senator's constituents regardless of the original Constitutional charter of the U.S. Senate. Today, the famous and the wealthy, those who could potentially contribute the most to a senatorial re-election campaign, may garner more of a senator's attention than the average constituent.

In some cases, the individual citizen advocate may be a journalist. Journalists, and the media in general, are a unique case of special interests.

Media

What differentiates the media from other special interests is that the media does not need to depend on lobbyists to advance their agenda. Nor does the media need to bother to meet with senators or other leaders – although they certainly do so. The media is positioned to bypass the entire lobbying scene and can attempt to advance its agenda indirectly by influencing the electorate. So-called journalists can spin a story based on their bias in subtle ways to attempt to tilt the outcome of a controversial issue, vote or election in their favor.

The media has always had an important role in the conduct of our affairs, but the national media has grown in influence and power since 1913. While technological advances established the infrastructure for today's national media, the 17th Amendment provides the political power that sustains it. The electorate depends on the media for information on the activities and votes of senators (and other elected officials).

The founding fathers chose to limit the influence of the media indirectly. While they explicitly codified free speech and the freedom of the press in the Bill of Rights (in the First Amendment), they also insulated the Senate from pressure that could otherwise be exerted by the media. The press could report whatever they wanted about a senator or the Senate with little or no influence on a Senate vote since each senator was beholding to his state's legislature. A state legislature is much less likely to bend to national public opinion or political correctness.

Cooling of the Process

In fact, the Senate is not fulfilling one of the primary intentions of the founding fathers; that is to "cool" the legislative process.

From the official federal government website[3] detailing the history of the Senate:

---

[3] www.senate.gov/artandhistory/history/minute/Senate_Created.htm

"In selecting an appropriate visual symbol of the Senate in its founding period, one might consider an anchor, a fence, or a saucer. Writing to Thomas Jefferson, who had been out of the country during the Constitutional Convention, James Madison explained that the Constitution's framers considered the Senate to be the great "anchor" of the government. To the framers themselves, Madison explained that the Senate would be a "necessary fence" against the "fickleness and passion" that tended to influence the attitudes of the general public and members of the House of Representatives. George Washington is said to have told Jefferson that the framers had created the Senate to "cool" House legislation just as a saucer was used to cool hot tea."

The "fickleness and passion" of the House is primarily due to the pressure and influence of the media and our pop culture. Today's culture is content with sound bites and seems to avoid in-depth analysis of serious issues in favor of emotion-based or "feel good" politics. Many of our debates today are decided on emotion and the success of derisive or condescending remarks intended to diminish political opposition to the mainstream media agenda. Emotion is a terrible substitute for serious analysis when determining public policy. We see many negative and unintended consequences of our public policy decisions because legislative initiatives are not fully considered and vetted for our long-term national interests. Outcomes of poorly conceived initiatives are often judged by the mainstream media based on intentions and not factual performance.

Today, since senators are popularly elected, the Senate is subject to the same media and cultural pressures as the House. It is no longer positioned to cool the legislative process and often, we see the Senate or senators heating up the process un-necessarily. Usually, it is a senator, not a member of the House, who is being interviewed on television and the outspoken senator is typically advancing an emotional appeal for support of a controversial cause.

Senators from both sides of the political aisle will often take the mainstream media position on many issues because senators rely on the media for re-election. Intentionally and overtly taking the opposing side of an issue virtually guarantees the senator will suffer a maelstrom of bad press in the national news and lampooning by late night entertainers. This type of bad press can negatively impact a senator's prospects for re-election. So, in a very real sense, senators are discourage from doing the right thing when it requires them to deviate from the prevailing view of the national media.

Since the 17th Amendment, the media's influence has grown and unfortunately, they've proven that they cannot be trusted with this responsibility. Most media organizations have a specific worldview and an agenda that they routinely attempt to advance. Interestingly, most "journalists" don't bother to engage issues in detail. Instead, they have found ways to advance their view point and their agenda in subtle ways by carefully selecting their words and their presentation of "facts". Often, they resort to denigrating the opposing view or the character of the person holding this view. This mainstream media agenda is ideologically-based and this ideology is not necessarily consistent with our long-term national interests.

The media not only acts to advance an agenda and influence an outcome of an issue, they also provide support to favored political candidates. The media uses its influence to get favored senators re-elected and un-favored ones defeated. There is no doubt media bias existed prior to 1913, but the media's influence in this regard prior to 1913 would have been limited (since senators were appointed rather than popularly elected).

Watchdogs

Unlike the people of a state whom are dependent on the media, members of the state legislature had the time and interest to closely monitor the activities and voting records of their two senators. Each state legislature was a watch-dog group of sorts, ever suspicious of federal government activities and doggedly watchful of their senators in Washington, D.C. State legislatures were guardians of their own interests and the interests of the people.

James Madison, in Federalist #26, wrote:

> "...the State legislatures, who will always be not only vigilant but suspicious and jealous guardians of the rights of the citizens against encroachments from the federal government, will constantly have their attention awake to the conduct of the national rulers, and will be ready enough, if anything improper appears, to sound the alarm to the people, and not only to be the VOICE, but, if necessary, the ARM of their discontent."

The 17th Amendment severed the relationship between senators and the legislatures of each state. State legislatures are no longer positioned to be our guardians, the voice or the arm of our discontent.

Senator Diplomats

For a politician to gain sufficient support within a state legislature to secure the appointment, a senatorial candidate would have needed to be a diplomat. Most state legislatures are roughly divided between two political parties. An "extremist" may not appeal to a sufficient number of state-level legislators on both sides of the aisle to secure the appointment. Rather than attempting to divide the electorate (as we so often see today), a senator would likely have the temperament and skills needed to bring people together – a true statesman.

A majority of the people of any state can easily be fooled by their senator over a six-year term especially if the senator acts like a statesman and the media provides support in the form of positive press.

Accountability

After securing the appointment, senators would have needed to both listen to and tactfully educate their "constituents" in state-level government so federal initiatives would have been understood.

Imagine a time when a senator could meet with all of his constituents (i.e., state senators and representatives) at one time in one room (i.e., at the state capitol). Imagine being able to discuss the nuances of an issue, ask questions, answer questions and hammer out differences to reach a consensus position to take back to Washington, D.C. This probably didn't always occur due to the personalities involved or other factors, but imagine the possibility. Imagine how much "cooler" the legislative process in Washington, D.C. could be. Imagine how much more accountability the senator would be to his state's constituents (i.e., the state legislators). These state legislators would be highly informed constituents who would likely hold their senators up to a very high standard of behavior and performance.

Today we see all sorts of behavior by U.S. senators. They are typically on their best behavior when vying for re-election, but even during re-election they are no longer fulfilling their (original) Constitutional charter of advancing the interests of their states or the nation. Often, campaigning causes them to deviate even further from this charter as they make promises of grandiose federal giveaway programs that we can't afford. It certainly isn't in the interests of the several states to have such a large (expansive) and expensive federal government since it can cripple our national economy, devalue our currency and negatively affect state-level initiatives.

Once elected (or re-elected), senators will often advance legislation to fulfill these campaign promises. Of course, they must find ways to fund these new or expanded programs, but there are always funding or enactment options. Mandates to the states by the federal government is one good option from the perspective of federal politicians since it permits them to fulfill promises without driving up our national debt. The popular election of senators not only affects the relationship

24

between senators and the states, it also affects the relationship between the federal government and the states.

State Mandates

Since the states no longer have a voice at the federal level, it is now possible and not altogether uncommon for the federal government to mandate programs and spending by the states. Short of filing a lawsuit against the federal government, the states are powerless to stop these mandates. This type of state mandate was much less likely to be enacted prior to the 17th Amendment since the Senate would have been much less likely to support such a mandate.

When the federal government mandates spending on a program by the states, state-level budgets have to be adjusted to fund the new mandate and other, perhaps more worthwhile programs have to be scaled back or defunded altogether.

State Homogenization

These state mandates and the myriad of federal regulations tend to homogenize our nation beyond the intention of our framers. Under federalism, states should be free to experiment. Our nation of states should be conducting 50 state-level experiments in healthcare, taxation, business regulations, etc. States should be learning from one another based on the outcome of these experiments.

While the states experiment, residents are free to migrate from one state to another as the results of these experiments become evident. A shrinking labor force and tax base can force a state to re-examine its policies relative to other, similar states. In a very real sense, these experiments keep the states "honest" and force them towards good public policies.

These state-level experiments are being thwarted by the federal government. When the federal government issues its decrees, all states, all businesses and all individuals must fall into compliance. The opportunity to experiment at the state-level is squashed or at least diminished.

More often than not, the federal decree should also be considered experimental since there is uncertainty about the outcome. Inevitably, there are unintended consequences and these are often negative.

Experimentation at the federal level can wreak havoc on all states and all people. Individuals are no longer free to migrate since there is nowhere to migrate to unless they are willing to emigrate out of the United States altogether. Emigration is an extreme option, but it is becoming more popular in recent years. You can probably guess why this would be the case.

As the federal government takes control over more and more aspects of our lives, bureaucrats in Washington decree how things will be done regardless of whether it is the best way or even a good way to accomplish the intended objective. Of course, this presumes the federal objective is worthwhile or even appropriate. In many cases, it is not.

Balance of Power

The Constitution was designed to restrict the federal government and only authorizes it to perform certain functions. The original structure of the Constitution established safeguards against a large, out-of-control federal government. These safeguards included the distribution of power. Power was divided between the federal government, the states and the people. This division of power is encapsulated in the 10th Amendment of the U.S. Constitution which states:

"The powers not delegated to the United States by the Constitution, nor prohibited by it to the States, are reserved to the States respectively, or to the people."

Power at the federal level was further separated between the three branches of government; the executive, legislative and judicial branches. The primary purpose of the legislative branch (i.e., the

Congress) is to write the laws. The executive branch (i.e., the president) is the final approval authority for new legislation and is charged with enforcing the laws. The judicial branch (i.e., the courts) interprets the laws. All three branches are responsible for ensuring the constitutionality of a law. The founding fathers expected this separation of power to constrain the initiatives of any one branch especially since the legislative branch included representatives from both the states and the people.

The original Constitutional structure established that high standard where a bill had to be in the interests of a majority of the people's representatives as well as a majority of the states and this interest was validated by the president before it became a law. This high standard worked as an important safeguard against passing laws that were unconstitutional.

When the states controlled the Senate, the 10th Amendment was well-defended against encroachments by the federal government.

Prior to the 17th Amendment, the Supreme Court could also be relied upon to rule on the Constitutionality of law in good faith. Now the court is being stacked with those who are willing to abrogate the Constitution in favor of efforts to expand the roles and authority of the federal government.

Beyond the Creation of Laws

Confirmation of Nominees

The Senate has other constitutional duties beyond the creation of laws (or bills). The first to be considered here is the confirmation of Supreme Court nominees.

The Supreme Court is now stacked with a number of justices who promote an ideology over the Constitution. The stacking of the Supreme Court is also due to the influence of special interests made possible by the 17th Amendment. Over the last few decades, it has become common practice for senators to apply various "litmus tests" as they consider Supreme Court and other federal court nominees.

Typically, these litmus tests are an evaluation to determine whether the views of the nominee are consistent with the political party of the senator. Once again, we see special interests trump the interests of the states and the politicization of the process to confirm federal nominees.

Most states may only be concerned whether a judicial nominee can read, understand and faithfully interpret the Constitution and our systems of laws as originally intended. Of particular interest is whether the nominee understands the overall premise of the Constitution as encapsulated in the 10th Amendment. This type of state interest doesn't seem to garner much attention anymore at the federal level since it isn't in the interests of those in Washington.

Impeachment

While the Senate has a direct and important role in the confirmation of nominees to federal posts, it also has a role in their removal from office. Once impeached, the Senate is charged with conducting a trial to determine whether the public servant should be removed from office. These impeachment trials may be conducted for many federal-level posts up to and including the president. Many may remember the Senate trial after the impeachment of President Clinton.

The politicization of the Senate and the fact that the Senate now advances special interests rather than state interests was evident in President Clinton's trial. Despite the careful preparation by House members to prosecute President Clinton, the Senate did not take their role, the trial or the charges seriously. Whether or not President Clinton should have been removed from office isn't the point. The Senate should have treated the trial with the care and respect it and the American people deserved. The manner in which this trial was conducted was an injustice to the states and the American people.

Expulsion

Expulsion is the term used to describe the involuntary removal of a senator from office by a vote of the Senate. The Constitution specifically includes an expulsion provision within Article I, Section 5. The Constitution does not specify the grounds for expulsion.

As one can imagine, the vote for the expulsion of a senator is now more likely to be governed by political party loyalties rather than national or state interests or even to protect the integrity of the Senate. The 17th Amendment perverts the integrity of the Senate on virtually every vote of consequence.

In addition to expulsion, senators are also subject to impeachment and removal from office, but this requires action by both Houses of Congress (see impeachment discussion above).

When the Constitution was being drafted, there was also consideration of a provision for the recall of senators by the state legislatures, however this recall provision was not included in the Constitution as ratified by the states. This may have been a mistake.

When a state legislature appointed a U.S. senator prior to 1913, this was essentially the hiring of a special envoy or ambassador. Does it make sense to hire this person and send him to Washington, D.C. for the next six years with no authority to fire this person for misconduct or other egregious behavior?

The omission of this recall provision has been interpreted at the federal level as meaning that senators, once appointed, were officers of the federal government and, therefore, not subject to recall by their state legislatures. The federal government's interpretation is that the removal of a senator from office is the exclusive domain of the U.S. government.

If we repeal the 17th Amendment, we should also consider a recall provision to enhance the relationship (and accountability) of senators to their home states. This recall provision does not need to specify the criteria or specific grounds for a recall; this could be determined by each state.

Treaties

Aside from these types of personnel decisions, the Senate also considers treaties. As the representatives of the states at the federal level, when the Senate votes on a treaty, the treaty should only be ratified if it is in the interests of a majority of the states (i.e., state governments). We don't see this type of consideration given to treaties either. Instead, we often see senators advancing the interests of their political party during these debates by making assertions that the treaty will result in jobs leaving the country or that the treaty will be good for the economy. Is it just coincidence that all states "represented" by Senate Democrats fall on one side of a treaty debate and all the states represented by Republican senators happen to fall on the other? Or, is this another disconnect between states and their Senate representation?

Declaration of War

The Senate also votes on declarations of war. The reader will note that there has not been a formal declaration of war since December 1941 when Japan insisted we enter WWII. It isn't that we haven't been engaged in any military conflicts. Is it possible that the solemn responsibility associated with the decision to engage in war has also been politicized?

The lack of a declaration of war since 1941 could be due to the politicization of the Senate or the distortion of the federal framework caused by the 17th Amendment. Is the fact that the states no longer have a voice in Washington, D.C. a factor? As the promoter of special interests, can the Senate be trusted with the responsibility to decide whether military intervention is in our long-term national interests? Should the president confer with the Senate before he decides to take military action?

Presidents may have a legitimate reason not to trust the Senate on this point. Senators today can only be entrusted to advance the interests of their political party, yet the several states certainly have an interest in whether the nation declares war or initiates military action. The Senate should be advancing these state and national interests, not those of the two major political parties.

The use of the military to impose our national will on another sovereign nation should never be taken lightly. The decision to commit

30

our sons and daughters, to put them in harm's way, carries a tremendous responsibility. Do we trust our president to make this decision alone? He is the Commander-in-Chief of our military, but this title or role does not grant the authority to decide whether to initiate military action against another sovereign nation. The question of war is reserved to the Congress. As Commander-in-Chief, the president decides how the military objectives will best be achieved once the question of war has been decided by the Congress. The War Powers Resolution of 1973 is a systemic maladjustment precipitated by the 17th Amendment.

Despite the authority granted to the president under the War Powers Resolution, entrusting one person with the power to make such a momentous decision on behalf of the entire United States is incongruent with our national character and does not adequately protect the interests of the United States (or our neighbors around the world) against presidential misconduct.

How many conflicts would we have avoided over the last hundred years if the states had voice in these decisions? Korea? Vietnam? Iraq? Afghanistan? Lebanon? Kosovo? Grenada? Libya? Panama? Bosnia? Somalia? Haiti? Were each of these conflicts advancing the interests of a majority of states? Were any of them?

After 9-11, President Bush did receive Congressional support for the Gulf War from both political parties, so perhaps this vote would have turned out the same, but one has to wonder. Did members of both political parties sense public support and vote accordingly? Was this a case of political expediency? If so, could a proper Senate have "cooled" the process? In the years since this vote, many Congressional members have distanced themselves from their vote of support providing evidence that this may have been a case of political expediency.

Military conflicts seem less likely without the 17th Amendment. Today, we often seem to rush to a military solution without careful consideration of our long-term national interests or even the specific objectives for the military action. We need a proper Senate to cool the process.

Judicial Branch

It isn't just the president and the Congress working together to grow the size, scope and reach of the federal government. The judicial branch isn't helping us to curb the federal power-grab either. A casual review of historical court cases reveals a disappointing and disturbing track record. Judges often cite one of the first ten amendments (i.e., the Bill of Rights) in their rulings. They parse the various clauses of these amendments or even of the basic Constitution without considering the overall premise of the document. These rulings often seem to be a deliberate re-interpretation of very short clauses within the Constitution to justify an expanded role of the federal government in defiance of the premise (and intent) of the Constitution.

> *Justices often parse the various clauses of the Constitution while ignoring the overall premise of the document.*

The Supreme Court justices are appointed for life. While some believe this does not work in our favor, the original intent was to insulate these justices from media and social pressure. Judges are supposed to be free to interpret the law outside of the political sphere. This was one additional measure enacted by our founding fathers to ensure that each branch would uphold its obligation to the Constitution and the rule of law. The Supreme Court was to be insulated from the media and politics and free to defend the Constitution. Unfortunately, the politicization of the Senate and the advancement of special interests over our national interests, has expanded and now permeates the Supreme Court. The integrity of the entire system is collapsing before our eyes and the majority of those sitting on the court seem all too willing to precipitate the degradation or are content to monitor the fall.

The infiltration of politics into the decisions of the Supreme Court is at least partly due to the Senate confirmation process. As senators successfully apply their litmus tests to Supreme Court nominees, the court has become increasingly packed with justices determined to advance specific political agendas. The actual text and limitations of the Constitution have been largely ignored in recent years in favor of creating a new philosophy of law or legal theories designed to justify a reinterpretation to suit their desired objectives. As such, the Constitution is on the verge of losing all meaning. In the end, their ultimate desire may be to live in a country without a functional Constitution where they can assume a copious level of power. It has to make you wonder what type of country they want to leave their children and grandchildren. Our nation without a viable and coherent constitution would be a bleak and dangerous place.

The New Framework of Government

The framework of the U.S. government established in 1913 has virtually guaranteed an ever larger, ever more intrusive and powerful federal government both at home and abroad (it is no wonder why so many view the U.S. as imperialistic). The 17th Amendment weakened the separation of power by effectively removing the states from the legislative branch. Now, the temptation presented to presidents, senators and representatives to advance pet projects is too great. Charismatic leaders will take advantage of the systemic weakness to advance their special interests whether constitutional or not (or whether in our national long-term interests or not).

Instead of having the branches of power jealously protecting against unconstitutional laws, the system has degraded to the point that all three branches support one another to grow the federal government beyond the limits of the Constitution regardless of which political party is in power. The federal government now dwarfs all other entities in our nation by any meaningful measure and it is growing exponentially. The concept of federalism, wherein the states and the people control anything not specifically authorized to the federal government, is virtually defunct. This is unfortunate and is likely to lead to our demise as a nation as federal government bureaucrats experiment at our expense and impose excessive burdens on the states, our businesses and our personal lives.

Should We Jealously Guard the Constitution?

Do we believe in the concepts and precepts of our Constitution? Do we believe it is worthy of our protection? Or, do we believe that the Constitution is simply a historical document with no relevance today? Perhaps it is a "living" Constitution – a document open to interpretation (or misinterpretation) in any conceivable manner so as to advance the agenda of a special interest or ideology. Each of us needs to carefully consider which is correct. Each of us needs to decide what the Constitution means, its purpose and whether it is relevant to our lives today.

If our government is no longer bound by the Constitution as ratified and intended by those who wrote and amended the document, then it has lost all meaning and we have lost our protection from the federal government. We are no longer guaranteed to live in a free nation. We will likely become servants or serfs of an increasingly tyrannical government. We can already see the signs.

Presidents now feel empowered to choose which laws to enforce, which to ignore and even create laws unilaterally. We have had a number of presidents who have issued executive orders when they fail to amass the political support of the legislative branch for the passage of a law. These executive orders are often in conflict with our long-term national interest and may subvert our individual liberties. The role of president has evolved into its own legislative branch.

Presidents may now feel free to use the Internal Revenue Service (IRS) or other agencies as weapons against their political opposition. Evidence suggests that the federal employees of the IRS (i.e., public servants) are willing to exploit the power of the agency for political purposes.   Cases abound where the IRS acts as accuser, law enforcement, prosecutor, judge and jury to seize property without actual due process.   It does not appear that this type of overreach is limited to the IRS either.

In recent years, several agencies (and individuals) have been accused of using the power of the government to advance their own interests to the detriment of the nation-at-large. Aside from this type of malfeasance, the evidence suggests that we are witnessing the systemic establishment of a class of politicians who are above the law.   This portends a more intrusive and even tyrannical federal government and it isn't likely to get better due to the results of the next election.

Liberty

As the federal government grows in scope and power, our individual liberties diminish. We are no longer considered to be the world's freest people and rightfully so.   The federal government doesn't just mandate policy or programs to the states, it also restricts individual choices, confiscates property and mandates what we must do with property. It also obligates us to support causes we wouldn't otherwise support.

When you become aware of a cause, you are free to support the cause with your time or financial support.   Whether it is for breast cancer awareness or research, feeding the hungry or community beautification, you are free to provide the type of support you wish or you may reject the cause for whatever reason. Causes can range from non-profit organizations to a specific family or even an individual. You can even send additional money to the federal government to pay down the debt if this is your desire. You decide how to spend your time and money.

When activists are able to successfully lobby the federal government to support a cause, it is no longer a voluntary act for individuals to support it. The cause will be funded with your tax dollars regardless of how vehemently you might object to the cause or whether you believe the cause to be morally reprehensible.

If you are an activist with a cause, and if you can wrangle federal support for your cause, this is still a great country. The rest of us suffer a degree of tyranny as a result of your success.

Problem Solving

Most causes are focused on solving (or at least addressing) a problem of one kind or another. It is important to realize that the federal government is not designed to solve every problem in our lives. Unfortunately, not everyone agrees with this assertion or, at least, not everyone agrees with which problems it should and shouldn't solve. Certainly not everyone will agree with a given federal solution. When the states have a voice in Washington, D.C., it becomes less likely that the federal government would attempt to solve problems outside of its purview.

Financial Soundness & Property Rights

The 17th Amendment was a subtle, yet profound change to the structure of the federal government that affected numerous relationships and introduced the opportunity for the influence of special interests. The 16th Amendment also affected relationships and also contributed to the growth of the federal government in both reach and power.

Some believe that the 16th Amendment is un-necessary and was politically motivated after a Supreme Court ruling struck down a direct tax that was not properly apportioned. Direct federal taxes on individuals were permissible prior to the 16th Amendment, however, they had to be levied based on the proportion of each state's population relative to that of the nation. Essentially, the 16th Amendment removed this original apportionment requirement for direct taxes.

Questions remain as to whether the 16th Amendment authorizes direct taxation on all forms of individual income. Regardless of intent or the legal authority of the 16th Amendment, it seems to have introduced significant ambiguity. The new Senate (established by the 17th Amendment) has been all too willing to exploit this legal ambiguity to grow the scope, reach and financial power of the federal government.

The 16th & 17th Amendments established the framework to provide our federal government access to huge amounts of capital and with copious power. The federal government now wields enormous power, not simply due to the accessibility of cash but because of the source of this cash; individuals. Once this systemic relationship was established, it was much easier to incrementally expand the scope of these taxes and tax rates thereby expanding the power of the federal government.

A New World of Business

The Industrial Revolution established the technological framework for powerful capitalists. Men like Rockefeller, Carnegie and J. P. Morgan grew their respective businesses until they were classified as monopolists. These monopolists controlled a majority of the market in their respective industry. Many felt that the rich were too powerful and that they were taking advantage of consumers. The federal government was seen as the only entity with sufficient power to reign in these titans of industry.

Some advocates of the 16th Amendment pushed for the confiscation of the wealth of these industrialists. Presumably this wealth represented money unfairly taken from the common man. They claimed the new income tax would only be imposed on the most powerful. The common man would not be taxed – there was no need to do so.

Once the federal government was authorized to tax personal property, who would be taxed and by how much could be changed at will. History has demonstrated that the only real monopoly is the federal government.

This system now taxes many of us commoners. Unlike most of the policies of the Democratic Party, here they actually promote a policy more consistent with the original intent cited above. While they may not be advocating a reduction of taxes on the middle class, Democrats do promote higher taxes on the rich.

Republicans claim that this is a form of class warfare. They believe that the rich already pay their fair share (or more) and that everyone should contribute. After all, every citizen of the United States is a beneficiary of our military. Everyone benefits from law and order. Why shouldn't everyone contribute something?

Republicans are also concerned that as fewer and fewer are taxed and more and more people are added to the rolls of welfare programs, it becomes the financial interest of a majority of voters to expand these federal wealth redistribution programs and tax the most productive citizens even more (thereby reducing the incentive and motivation to work hard and take risks).

Our founding fathers took great care to avoid setting up a democracy. Historically, democracies fail because more and more voters advance their own interests to the detriment of national interests. As the welfare rolls grow and the recipients of welfare programs vote to elect politicians promising to tax the productive and provide expanded benefits, the prospects for a prosperous nation diminishes. Fewer and fewer productive citizens will be supporting larger numbers of welfare program beneficiaries with more generous benefits.

Even though our founding fathers established a democratic-republic and not a democracy, as we stray further from our Constitution, we think of ourselves more and more as a democracy. Once again, this diminishes our long-term prospects. Under a democratic-republic, we rely on our elected (and appointed) representatives to make informed decisions to advance our long-term interests. This plan and organizational structure was to mitigate the risk of the tyranny of a majority over a minority.

Our collective push towards democracy is actually resulting in a large measure of socialism primarily due to the "low-information" voters. Many in our nation today simply don't understand the dangers of socialism, or perhaps many simply don't care. *Why not fleece the rich as long as we are able?*

Socialism never works and will never work, yet we keep adopting many of the tenants of socialism. Obamacare is one of the more recent examples. Another example is the tax system.

Redistribution of Wealth

Many in our country advocate the use of the tax system to equalize outcomes. It is the "strategy" of our war on poverty – a war that is skillfully used by politicians to buy votes using taxpayer dollars. They often lament that it isn't fair that some make so much more money than others or that the percentage difference between their incomes is growing. What they don't bother to tell you is that this growing disparity is a natural (i.e., mathematical) outcome of a healthy economy driven by entrepreneurs and powered by innovation.

'Feel good' or emotion-based public policy is a poor substitute for sound, economic-based policy. Emotion-based public policies are diminishing our long-term prosperity and even our viability as a sovereign nation.

Often, politicians advance a concept of fairness with respect to tax policy. The rich should pay their "fair share". It isn't fair that some are rich while others are stuck in poverty. Assertions regarding fairness by politicians should be a red flag to voters.

Our government was not constituted as the arbiter of "fairness". Fairness typically depends on a person's point of view. There are many in this country who demand we use the force of government to "legally" extort from the upper one percent. It doesn't seem fair to them when a rich man doesn't share more and more of his good fortune while others struggle to survive.

While it may seem unfair to the poor that the rich have so much, will it seem fair to the business owner who worked 20 hours a day,

39

seven days a week for years to be forced to hand over thousands of dollars each year to someone who has not lifted a finger to help himself or his family opting instead to let the government (i.e., taxpayers) provide? What seems only fair to one is inherently unfair to another. It may be useful here to draw an important distinction between the concepts of fairness and justice.

While government was not intended to be the arbiter of fairness, it is the arbiter of justice. The difference is in the law and the purpose of the law. Laws should not be written based on someone's arbitrary "standard" of fairness, but to protect rights.

Reform of the Income Tax System

Many have been calling for the reform of our tax system. They believe our tax system is too complex. How many hours are wasted each year just reading IRS publications and filling out forms? These are hours that could be truly productive. Instead, these hours are spent by the head of every productive household in America in a futile attempt to determine their "fair share" of taxes based on some arbitrary and constantly changing standard of fairness. Of course this presumes that a single "Amount you Owe" number can be computed after these countless hours of work, however not even the tax code experts can agree on a single number for many tax returns.

The vast majority of tax return filings include line items that could be challenged due to differences in interpretation. All but the simplest of returns raise questions of legality. When tested, not even the experts can agree on a single "Amount you Owe" solution for relatively straight-forward tax returns. This level of complexity shouldn't be acceptable to anyone, and frankly, it should lead one to wonder whether there is some intentionality behind the entangled web of tax code.

One strategy of the tyrannical is to impose such a web of complex regulations that no one can possibly comply with them all.

While our current tax code is complex and confusing, these observations do not go far enough. Rather than reforming the current tax code, the individual income tax needs to be eliminated entirely.

Forcibly taking money from the rich does not truly help anyone's prosperity. Generally, the rich are the producers. They create jobs and innovate to produce wealth and prosperity for everyone. So, by taking from the rich, the federal government is hobbling our economy and the prosperity of everyone. As much as it may feel good to punish the rich with higher taxes, it isn't helpful to anyone including the middle class or those in poverty. It doesn't advance anyone's financial interests except the politicians, bureaucrats, political cronies and special interests in Washington, D.C.

For all of our discussion regarding an arbitrary standard of fairness, this is actually an invalid premise of fairness. There is nothing fair about government confiscation of private property. There are more appropriate avenues for raising sufficient funds to operate a fully functioning federal government that conforms to the scope authorized by the Constitution.

The Federal Reserve Act was not based on good public policy either.

The Federal Reserve Act & Elastic Credit

Like the 16th Amendment, the Federal Reserve Act introduced a new entity to our financial system which contributed to the expansion of the federal government. In fact, it may be one of the most significant legislative initiatives in the financial history of the United States. Despite its significance, many don't understand the Federal Reserve, what it does or how it does it.

There are many books on the operation of the Federal Reserve. It is not the intent of this pamphlet to dive deeply into the Federal Reserve, but the genesis of the Federal Reserve may be of interest in this overall discussion of the 1913 Solution. For years, historians believed that the impetus behind the central bank in this country was started by Midwestern businessmen.

An Indianapolis Monetary Convention was held in 1897 by Midwestern businessmen to address or advance the need for "elastic credit". Actually, this convention and many other conferences leading up to 1913 were a ruse intended to sway policy makers and "educate" the public about the supposed benefits of a central bank. This ruse was perpetrated by John D. Rockefeller, JP Morgan and their associates (and not Midwestern businessmen). It was a rather elaborate plan that solicited the help of business associates, academics and other authorities to influence politicians and the public-at-large.

The "elastic credit" concept promoted by these advocates would be managed by a central bank so as to counteract economic cycles, i.e., booms and busts. If we had a flexible credit mechanism, they reasoned, we could better control economic cycles.

Much of the efforts of these men were shrouded in secrecy and deception culminating in a secret trip to Jekyll Island, Georgia by a handful of men to draft the Federal Reserve bill in November of 1910. This bill effectively proposed the creation of a cartel, much like the oil cartel of the Mid-East, except this was a money cartel. The men who wrote the bill would be the operators and beneficiaries of this cartel.

Among the objectives of these men was to obtain an exclusive franchise (i.e., a monopoly) from the federal government to create money. This creation of money would not be backed by gold or anything of value. They would create money (or credit) out of nothing.

With the monopoly on the creation of money, this would eliminate any competition. The idea was brilliant at its core. This is an even better way to amass a fortune than running a railroad, steel or oil company. Why, this was even better than convincing the federal government to hand over its printing presses.

These initiators of the Federal Reserve also sought to extend their shroud of secrecy by excluding access to the financial books of the operation. They did not want to be subjected to audits by the federal government or any outside agency. As if they needed to ensure the success of the operation even more, they also established provisions to shift any (unlikely) losses to taxpayers. Lastly, they convinced Congress that the purpose of the bill was to protect the public. The plan was both audacious and brilliant – and it worked.

By 1913, newly elected President Wilson was pushing hard for Federal Reserve legislation claiming the need to wrestle control of the nation's finances away from the very titans of industry orchestrating the central bank movement. Whether Wilson was aware of the secret scheme or the culprits behind the scheme is unclear. President Wilson was an academic who had been writing about public policy matters for years. These industrialists may have been able to hoodwink Wilson and take advantage of an academic overconfidence. Wilson was either complicit in the plan or he fell headlong into their trap.

The movement for a central bank gained momentum largely due to the covert efforts of these industrialists and their colleagues. In December of 1913, the Federal Reserve Act became law and the Federal Reserve was born. Since then, the magnitude and the frequency of recessions (and depressions) has continued unabated. In fact, the Great Depression occurred just twenty years later.

The central bank sets the nation's monetary policy so as to avoid recession. These mysterious bankers purport to be apolitical and outwardly attempt to stay out of the political arena, but inevitably, they set monetary policy based on the performance of our economy. As the federal government enacts legislation and regulations that retard economic growth, the Federal Reserve adjusts the amount of liquidity in the system or uses other tools at its disposal to attempt to re-ignite the economy and (hopefully) counteract the bad public policies imposed by Washington, D.C. This effectively compensates for federal initiatives that are a burden on our prosperity thereby enhancing the re-election prospects for incumbent politicians. So, while the Federal Reserve purports to be apolitical, fulfillment of their charter results in a measure of political cover for incumbents.

This political cover costs us in many ways; the re-election of incumbents is but one. Many of the laws and regulations established over the last one hundred years have been a drag on our economy and limit our overall prosperity. Federal Reserve policies intended to compensate for a weak economy due to the burdens of the new federal government are ultimately inflationary. Inflation is a flat tax on us all. The political cover provided by the Federal Reserve comes at a price and it isn't cheap. Many don't realize the connection between the anti-business environment established by the federal government, our slow economic growth, the follow-up actions by the Federal Reserve and the resulting higher inflation.

Competing (& Sometimes Contradictory) Objectives

According to the Federal Reserve's website, the statutory objectives for its monetary policy are maximum employment, stable prices and moderate interest rates. During times of widespread unemployment, the Federal Reserve typically lowers interest rates and provides additional monetary liquidity to stimulate economic activity. This can destabilize prices.

Lowering interest rates to stimulate a sluggish economy during a period of already high inflation may not be the best monetary policy. With the so-called "dual mandate" of the Federal Reserve, sometimes one objective has to be subverted or demoted relative to another. Depending on the state of the economy, the Federal Reserve can't always pursue all of their statutory objectives simultaneously.

The Declining Value of the U.S. Dollar

Inflation is caused by monetary policy. Many economists and journalists today mistakenly believe that inflation is caused by a sustained increase in economic activity. Their theory is that the faster the economy grows, the higher the rate of inflation. Technically, this is not the case. There can be periods of sustained economic growth with deflation. The United States experienced this from 1865 to 1896. Milton Friedman wrote that *"Inflation is, always and everywhere, a monetary phenomenon."*

While inflation is a monetary phenomenon, higher economic growth may cause inflation to manifest sooner. Our lethargic growth since the great recession may be the only reason inflation has been relatively benign the last ten years, but the government and Federal Reserve have done their part to ensure that inflation will eventually explode.

For the first 124 years of our nation's history, inflation was almost non-existent. According to an Oregon State University (OSU) website[4], the value of a dollar decreased by less than 10% from 1789 to 1913. This is not a 10% per year average, but 10% total in 124 years. So, a dollar in 1789 was still worth over 90¢ in 1913.

In the 100 years following 1913, the value of the U.S. dollar has declined by an average annualized inflation rate of about 3.2%. This is not a 3.2% total over the entire 100 year period, but an average of 3.2% in each and every one of these 100 years. This may not sound significant, but it adds up. A dollar in 1913 had degraded to the point of being worth less than a nickel by 2013. While this may be considered a stable decline of value (consistent with the objective of stable prices), this is an abysmal record and represents another tax; a tax on savers.

This degradation of the U.S. dollar is a flat tax. Everyone who spends dollars today that were earned in the past is paying this flat tax. This hurts savers and discourages saving. Policies that promote inflation encourage spending and our consumption-based society. Investment experts often lament that we are not saving enough to fund our retirement, yet our monetary and tax policies discourage saving for the long-term. (Interestingly, policies that discourage saving for retirement generally increase dependence on government programs which also confers additional power and prestige to federal politicians.) Others lament our consumption-based economy, yet our inflationary policies virtually guarantee this outcome.

---

[4] http://liberalarts.oregonstate.edu/sites/liberalarts.oregonstate.edu/files/polisci/faculty-research/sahr/inflation-conversion/pdf/cv2013.pdf

Republican politicians generally promote the concept of a flat-tax, but decry inflation and inflationary policies. Democrat politicians denounce the concept of a flat tax as being regressive, but do not seem to mind enacting spending or other regulatory policies that will ultimately lead to inflation.

A flat tax is not regressive. Mathematically, a flat tax is fair. Graduated tax rates or schedules are arbitrary and inherently unfair. However, imposing a tax discourages the taxed behavior or activity. Discouraging people from working by imposing a flat income tax or discouraging savers by imposing an inflation-based flat tax on our currency are bad public policies that should be avoided.

Of course, the reason for our inflation policy is to make huge deficits more affordable for the federal government. When the federal government operates at a budgetary deficit, it has to either borrow, tax or print money to finance the deficit. Borrowing from the private sector drives up the cost of capital for businesses resulting in slower economic growth. Voting to increase taxes can be difficult for a politician's re-election prospects, so they tend to avoid doing so. The government can monetize the debt by printing more money, but this results in inflation. However, with inflation, the government can pay back the loan or service the debt with dollars that are worth less than the dollars originally borrowed and spent. Inflation makes debt more affordable for the government, so this becomes the preferred solution. Many in Washington, D.C. seem to believe that excessive spending and resulting debt is acceptable as long as it is paid for by future generations with dollars that are worth less.

Please don't let the current low-interest rate lull you into a sense of complacency. With $19 trillion of debt, the federal government, our nation, may be on the cusp of financial collapse even with inflation. Currently, interest rates are at historic lows, yet we have to budget $248 billion to service our national debt (within the $3.95 trillion FY2016 budget). If the Federal Reserve ever has to raise interest rates due to higher inflation, the service on our federal debt could quickly overwhelm our nation's financial capacity. The interest payments required on a $20 trillion loan at a 6% interest rate would amount to over $1 trillion each year. If interest rates rise to the 15% level of the early 1980s, our budget would need to include an additional $2.5 trillion for interest payments. Interest payments of $2 or $3 trillion within a $4 trillion budget should be considered significant even by the most hardened Keynesian politician.

Of course, if we borrowed to pay this additional interest, this would add another $1 trillion or more to our national debt increasing the amount of the interest that would need to be paid for each year thereafter. The federal government would need to borrow more and more at a faster (and higher) rate just to service our debt, never mind paying for all the federal workers and federal programs. As the government borrows or prints more money to pay this interest, inflation will increase even faster. This would likely get out of control very quickly with no easy way to stop the cycle.

The financial soundness of the USA is in serious jeopardy. We are already monetizing our debt in the sense that our government and the Federal Reserve are printing money to repay the interest of our current government loans and we are doing this during a time of interest rates at or near zero percent. This is not the basis of sound financial or currency management and it is likely to cause serious problems for our nation soon. We are facing tough times.

Austerity of the magnitude required to return the United States to financial solvency would likely require abandoning many federal programs including both "discretionary" and "non-discretionary" programs. This probably won't be welcomed by many who have come to expect government handouts. With a situation of forced austerity, our nation will likely face both internal and external threats and we will be in a weak position to counter or mitigate these threats.

We need to act and we need to act quickly to get our nation back on a sound financial foundation.

Proposed Solutions – USA 2.1?

So, if the 1913 Solution didn't work, what should we try next? There have been several solutions proposed to address the symptoms caused by the 1913 Solution.

Political Exemptions

We often see legislation that provides for exemptions for federal politicians from the rules the rest of us must follow. Today, we find that members of Congress have their own medical program (separate from Obamacare) and their own retirement program (separate from Social Security). This helps to explain the use of the now common phrase "the ruling class" when referring to members of the House and Senate. They have become not just a ruling class, but a class of high privilege. They pass one set of rules for us to follow while exempting themselves from these rules.

These ruling class exemptions have led to proposals for a Constitutional amendment to eliminate these types of political exemptions. However, this is yet another symptom of the 17th Amendment and the 1913 Solution.

If a Constitutional amendment were ratified that successfully forced the ruling class to comply with all laws as common citizens, this still would not align the interests of senators with those of the states or the nation. Senators would still be free to advance special interests; although they may not be able to overtly advance their own (personal) financial interests. This type of amendment only addresses one narrow aspect (or symptom) of the 17th Amendment. The repeal of the 17th Amendment should automatically address this particular symptom since senators would not be as free to advance their personal financial interests.

While this type of amendment may have merit, ratification should only be considered after the repeal of the 17th Amendment and only if the amendment was still deemed necessary to restore good governance. The Constitution should only be altered to the extent needed to re-establish a system of good governance and no more.

Term Limits

Periodically, we hear of a suggestion to limit the number of terms a federal-level politician can serve. By limiting the number of terms, they reason we would be less apt to have career politicians and a permanent ruling class.

The various symptoms of the 1913 Solution make term limits an attractive solution for many. Keep in mind that even if term limits were enacted, the Senate would still be free to promote special interests and would not be forced to advance the interests of their states or the nation. Term limits might help slow the destruction of our nation, but would not reverse the damage already wrought or save us from eventual demise. Our objective needs to be to restore our nation to health, not just to place it on life-support so as to slow its eventual death. A repeal of the 17th Amendment would better meet the long term objectives sought by those who promote the term limits approach.

Even within the minimum alteration approach mentioned at the end of the previous section, a simple repeal of the 17th Amendment is probably not adequate. Instead we should also consider including a provision for the recall of senators by the respective state legislature. This would increase the accountability of senators to their (home) state legislature. Those in the state legislatures probably aren't too keen on senators who advance rules and programs from which U.S. senators are exempt but state legislators and the other state residents must follow. After all, these senators should be addressing the needs of their state and the nation – not advancing their own, personal interests. Service within the U.S. Senate ought to be a position of honor and privilege – not the privilege of enacting laws for self-enrichment, but the privilege to serve the nation with a humble heart.

Campaign Finance Reform

A repeal of the 17th Amendment also alleviates the need for campaign finance reform. Much of the money raised and spent by federal candidates is on Senate races. In fact, contemporary Senate races have nationwide implications. Solicitations for Senate races now cross state borders. Many of us are asked to contribute to senatorial candidates in other states. Why should voters or interests in other states have such an influence on a senatorial race in your state? This ought to be a concern for the resident of every state. This type of big-business political machinery is another indication of the importance of each senatorial race.

If outside-the-state solicitations for a senatorial race in your state is not sufficiently concerning, consider the allegations that some Senate races have accepted contributions from foreigners or foreign governments. This possibility ought to be a great concern to all of us.

According to opensecrets.org, the average cost of a winning 2014 senatorial campaign was in the neighborhood of $7 million. It is important to realize that each of these winners also had challengers who may have raised and spent a nearly comparable amount.

While senatorial candidates may feel great temptation to accept donations from foreign sources, there are only a few reasons for a foreign concern to contribute money to a senatorial election campaign (and there is no good reason for the politician to accept the donation). These nice foreigners could be just generous and charitable with no expectation of anything in return, however this type of contribution certainly suggests the possibility of buying influence. Imagine a foreign government or foreign nationals influencing Senate votes on treaties, tariffs or even the authorization to sell weapons or technology to the influential nation.

It is no wonder why campaign finance reform has been a popular initiative over the years. We have strayed very far from the original precepts of the Senate and the days when senators were selected within the state capitols across our own nation.

With the repeal of the 17th Amendment, senators would no longer have a need to raise funding for a popular election. The race between senatorial candidates would once again be conducted within the confines of each state's capitol building.

Beyond Campaign Finance Reform and Term Limits, there are other proposals out there and the Texas Plan is one worthy of consideration.

The Texas Plan

Texas Governor Greg Abbott wrote a pamphlet entitled "Restoring the Rule of Law; With the States Leading the Way". This pamphlet (referred to as "The Texas Plan") is very well written and includes a wealth of historical information.   Gov. Abbott proposes nine Constitutional Amendments to restore the rule of law:

I.   Prohibit Congress from regulating activity that occurs wholly within one State.

II.   Require Congress to balance its budget.

III. Prohibit administrative agencies — and the unelected bureaucrats that staff them — from creating federal law.

IV.   Prohibit administrative agencies — and the unelected bureaucrats that staff them — from preempting state law.

V.   Allow a two-thirds majority of the States to override a U.S. Supreme Court decision.

VI.   Require a seven-justice super-majority vote for U.S. Supreme Court decisions that invalidate a democratically enacted law.

VII.   Restore the balance of power between the federal and state governments by limiting the former to the powers expressly delegated to it in the Constitution.

VIII.   Give state officials the power to sue in federal court when federal officials overstep their bounds.

IX.   Allow a two-thirds majority of the States to override a federal law or regulation.

While Governor Abbott's proposals are worthy of consideration, without a repeal of the 17th Amendment, we are still addressing the symptoms without fixing the root cause foisted on us by the 17th or the other provisions of the 1913 Solution.

For example, the Texas Plan proposes a balanced budget amendment (item #II). While an amendment requiring a balanced budget certainly has merit, unless the 17th Amendment is repealed, Congress would likely raise taxes or find other avenues for spending (e.g., more state mandates) or they will employ various accounting tricks to circumvent the intent.

The Texas Plan also proposes an amendment to strengthen the 10th Amendment and authorize the several states the power to sue the federal government in court whenever the federal government oversteps its authority (item #VIII). If the Senate is still controlled by special interests and political parties, the result of this proposed change may be a never-ending parade of state lawsuits in federal court. Granting the states the authority to sue the federal government is an idea worthy of merit, but why not fix the systemic problem that leads to these 10th Amendment encroachments?

> *If the 17th Amendment is meaningless, then why keep it?*
>
> *If it serves a purpose, what is it?*

Proposal items V through IX of the Texas Plan also appear to address symptoms related to the 17th Amendment. Each of these proposals may be worthy of consideration, but we should only do so after the 17th Amendment is repealed. Otherwise, we are not addressing the root cause.

Addressing the Root Cause – USA 3.0

There are many other examples of proposed solutions and Constitutional Amendments to address the myriad of symptoms caused by the 1913 Solution. One of the first precepts of problem solving is to clearly identify and define the problem. Accurately defining the problem provides the foundation for determining the root cause of the problem. Addressing the root cause provides the only chance of solving the actual problem. Solve the actual problem and these other symptoms will eventually be resolved. The 1913 Solution is the root cause of many of the problems we are dealing with today.

The Repeal of 1913...

With a better understanding of the ramifications of the 16th and 17th Amendments and the Federal Reserve Act, some might conclude we need to repeal 1913 – the entire year. Wipe it off the books. This probably would take an act of Congress.

While a repeal of a calendar year is not likely, one of the beautiful aspects of the Constitution is that we don't need federal government involvement to repeal the 16th and 17th Amendments.

> *If the 17th Amendment was intended to alleviate the under representation of states in the Senate, it failed. Now **no** state is represented in Washington, D.C.*

Article V of the Constitution provides for two pathways for amending the Constitution. In the past, Congress has initiated the amendment process, but this is not likely in these cases since it isn't in their interests to do so. Article V also states that a Constitutional convention may be convene by approval of two-thirds of the states (32 of 50). Once convened, a vote of approval by three-fourths of the states (38 of 50) are needed to ratify any proposed Constitutional amendment. This is a more difficult standard (or pathway) than the typical Article V approach initiated by Congress.

However, since a repeal of the 17th Amendment is consistent with the interests of the states, there is reason to be optimistic in the possibility of a Constitutional convention and an amendment to repeal the 17th. However, there is also reason to believe that a repeal of the 17th would be a difficult battle due to the opposition we'd likely face.

Opposition to the Repeal of the 17th

Some in our nation would recoil at the very suggestion of a repeal of the 17th Amendment. Many like having a federal government that has sufficient power to enact their agenda. From their perspective, it is much easier to advance their agenda with a federal government open to special interest influence and powerful enough the force the rest of us into compliance (or submission). A repeal of the 17th Amendment is not in their interests and those involved in advancing special interests who understand the importance of the 17th Amendment relative to their business model will likely stop at nothing to block its repeal. U.S. Senators and the national media are squarely in this faction. This makes a repeal a much bigger challenge, but again, we only need to convince the legislators (and conventioneers) of 38 states.

The opponents of a repeal could adopt a few general strategies. First, a repeal of the 17th Amendment could be characterized as either meaningless or a waste of time. Hopefully, the discussion herein convinces you otherwise, but if not, then you should demand to know why we should keep the 17th. A repeal of the 17th Amendment is only meaningless if the 17th itself is meaningless. But if the 17th Amendment is meaningless, then why keep it? If it adds value to our system of government, then demand to know how. If there is value-added by the 17th Amendment, we need to understand this value. It is not obvious or apparent.

The second strategy 17th Amendment defenders might take is to argue that prior to 1913, some state legislatures were deadlocked and could not appoint a senator. These states, they would argue, were not represented in Washington, D.C.

While true, only these states suffered, not the entire nation. The original system encouraged state legislatures to resolve their own problem. After all, these states were either not represented or were under-represented in the U.S. Senate. The governor and other state leaders would have applied pressure to the legislature to appoint a new senator(s).

While some might argue that prior to 1913, some states were under-represented, since the 17th Amendment was ratified, _no_ state has been represented in Washington, D.C. The 17th Amendment did not solve this problem in any manner and in fact, it exacerbated the problem to the extreme. Now none of our 50 states are represented.

The 17th Amendment as a solution to this problem did not employ one of the most important steps in problem solving by answering the question, "Whose problem is it?" In this case, it was a state problem, not a federal problem. As we've learned over the years, solving state

---

Enhancing the Relationship between
Senators & State Legislatures

Beyond a repeal of the 17th Amendment and the enactment of a recall provision, there are other ways to enhance the relationship between the state legislatures and their appointed senators. One worth considering would be to have each state pay for the salaries and benefits of their two senators out of the state budget. Aside from making it abundantly clear to whom senators report, removing senators from the federal payroll also eliminates the conflict of interest inherent in the current system.

Under the current system, senators and representatives vote on budget resolutions that include their own salary and benefits. Furthermore, barring a veto and override, the president must sign the budget bill for it to become law. This provides the president some political leverage over the Senate and the House. Removing senators' paychecks from this equation would keep the salaries of representatives and federal bureaucrats at-large in-check. Senators would be less likely to approve a budget with salary increases for their colleagues in the House if their own salaries are based on their state's economic performance. Without Senate support, no bill becomes law.

---

problems at the federal level does not work well and tends to exacerbate all of our problems.

The 17th may have been enacted due to this state under-representation problem, but it is more likely to have been a populist effort to shift power to the common man. Remember that in the early 20th century, the socio-economic impacts of the Industrial Revolution were being fully realized and not all of these impacts were positive. Some corporations were seen as being bigger and more powerful than the federal government and this was considered to be problematic. Working conditions at many factories and meat processing facilities were deplorable giving rise to workers' unions. Many believed the federal government needed to take action to exert some control over corporations to ensure safe, healthy working conditions and to ensure fair competition.

The Progressive Party platform in 1912 called for a "self-controlled democracy" and supported the direct election of senators[5]. Teddy Roosevelt wanted to give everyone a "Square Deal". The 17th Amendment may have been an initiative to fix our nation's problems by moving towards a direct democracy.

While this shift of power to the individual may have been the rationale for the 17th Amendment, it fails in this regard also. The 17th did shift some modicum of power to the individual, but from a system-level perspective, the power was so dispersed to a group so ill-informed, that the amendment did not provide the systemic change desired. Senators were no longer likely to be held accountable and they soon realized they were liberated to advance whatever special interest they desired. Furthermore, the states were no longer positioned to protect the people as Madison envisioned. The 17th may have been based on a good and noble intention, but it did not effectively solve any of our nation's problems. Instead, it enacted a new structure of

---

[5] Richard L. Watson Jr., *The Development of National Power; The United States 1900-1919*, Boston: Houghton Mifflin, 1976, 147

government that caused many more problems for the people, the states and the nation at-large. It is time we learned from this mistake and fix the systemic, structural problems created by the 17th Amendment.

Others might argue that it would be too difficult to repeal the 17th Amendment and not worth the effort. Hopefully the discussion herein quells any question of potential benefit and convinces those doubters that the expended effort would be worthwhile. The future prosperity and even the future existence of the United States likely depends on its repeal.

Opponents to the repeal of the 17th Amendment might argue that it would usher in a heightened level of corruption. U.S. senators might be selected as a result of a corrupt process within a state's capitol.

Localized corruption confined to a state is better than the corruption we currently have at the national level. The current system is much more corrupt and easily corruptible than any level of corruption that could occur at the state level in terms of impact on our national interests.

Of course, the Constitutional Amendment to repeal the 17th could just as easily allow for alternative selection processes. We don't have to enact a simple repeal of the 17th Amendment and return to a straight-forward appointment by state legislatures. Each state could decide how their senators would be appointed. A governor could nominate a senatorial candidate and both the state House and Senate could vote on the nomination. The legislature could nominate and the governor could confirm. There are a number of ways states could establish for the appointment of their senators and the U.S. Constitution probably doesn't need to detail this process except that senators would be appointed by the respective state government. The wording of the Constitution should not permit the popular election of senators since this is antithetical to the overall objective. Senators must serve and must be accountable to their state government. This is the charter of the Senate and the job of each senator.

Another argument is that if we conduct a Constitutional Convention to consider a repeal of the 17th Amendment, there is no limit to the number of other amendments that could be proposed or the nature of these amendments. If most believe this is the primary objection to a convention, why not establish an agenda and ground rules that constrain the business of the convention to specific proposed amendments or subjects? Perhaps this type of limitation would assuage the concerns of a majority and open the door to a possible convention without unlimited risk. This is exactly the approach being taken by a 'Convention of States' movement.

The Convention of States[6] movement is pushing to conduct an Article V Constitutional Convention. This movement is limiting the proposed convention to three categories; fiscally restraining the federal government, restraining the power or scope of the federal government and term limits. Each proposed amendment considered at this convention must fall into one of these categories. At this point, it is unclear whether a repeal of the 17th Amendment would comply with these constraints and be eligible for consideration at this convention. Please join this movement and recommend that a repeal of the 17th Amendment be considered or the constraints modified to allow for its repeal.

A repeal of the 16th Amendment and the Federal Reserve Act would certainly fall within these categories and could be considered at this convention as currently structured.

Any amendment advanced by this or any other constitutional convention would need to be ratified by a vote by three-fourths of the states (38 states out of 50). This is a high standard and a good convention process executed by people operating in good faith with a sufficient knowledge base should be able to vet each proposed amendment.

---

[6] www.conventionofstates.com

Long-Term Prospects

Even with a repeal of the 17th Amendment, many of the symptoms will not simply vanish overnight. It may take years to realign the system and resolve the many issues that resulted from the 17th Amendment, but at least the systemic problem will have been resolved and the foundation for good government re-established.

Liberty vs Tyranny

Based on the number and scope of federal laws and regulations, there is no doubt we are losing our freedoms. The government is specifying to a greater degree how we are to conduct our businesses, our personal affairs and our lives. Various government agencies are used to impose the bureaucratic view on our lives; the IRS is one good example.

There are many credible allegations that the IRS is being used as a political tool (or weapon). Evidence suggests the IRS has been used to block applications for tax exempt status by grassroots organizations representing the political opposition.

How long before the healthcare system is also used as a political weapon to silence opposition? Publically disagree with the president and the next thing you know, your child's surgery is cancelled or your mother's plug is pulled. The prospect is worthy of profound concern.

New System? Hardly

Fully 80 percent of our nation are dissatisfied with Congress. Most people when asked, indicate they like their representative and senators. It is the Congressional members from other states with whom most are dissatisfied. In reality, it is our system that is broken. A very large number of seemingly unrelated symptoms have manifested, but the root cause is embedded in the 1913 Solution. We will only fix these systemic issues by addressing the root cause.

Only by repealing the 17th Amendment will we restore our nation's system of government. One of the most beautiful and elegant aspects of this proposed solution is that they are not new or untested. We've tried this solution before and it has been proven to work. For the first 124 years of our nation's history, this system was in-place. This isn't a solution dreamed up by the author of this pamphlet. This is the system of our founding fathers and it worked rather well for over a hundred years.

The decision makers of 1913 probably believed they were making changes to improve the United States. Hopefully, most who read this document are now convinced that these three changes were not improvements in our system of government. If this is the case, do we have the courage and the will to reverse these decisions and to return to the system of our founding fathers?

Objections

Assuming a few patriots are willing to advance these ideas, listen carefully to the nature of any ensuing criticism.

- Is the criticism directed at you, me or the idea being advanced?

- Does the critic focus on historical facts?

- Does the point negate the overall assertions advanced herein? Is the critic parsing a specific assertion within this document while ignoring the overall premise?

- Does the critic provide specific rationale on why the idea(s) are not worthy of consideration?

- Does the rationale provided make sense? Is it coherent?

- Can they defend the 17th Amendment on its own merits? What are the merits of the 17th Amendment?

- Who is making the argument against the repeal of the 17th? Is it a member of the mainstream media? Or a senator? Is it someone from a special interest organization? Remember the old adage to "follow the money."

Summary

On May 20th, 2016, the Wall Street Journal reported that consumer credit card debt was on-track to reach $1 trillion before the end of the year[7]. Obviously, this is a huge number and many pundits lament that so many of us are living beyond our means. Some have pointed out that we enslave ourselves when we borrow money. It may not be possible to conceptually understand a number of this magnitude and it is more than a little frightening to think of this level of indentured servitude for ourselves, our friends and our neighbors.

It is important to realize that this $1 trillion of credit card debt was amassed by a collection of 320 million Americans (or their guardians) in a more or less free market economy over many years. Not surprisingly, we amassed this personal debt while forced to surrender a large portion of our income each year to the federal government. One trillion dollars represents about one year of federal tax receipts (or tax revenues) collected from individuals. Arguably, this credit card debt would not exist without the 16th and 17th Amendments.

The federal government spent all of our taxes and still managed to amass an additional $19 trillion debt on our behalf. This federal debt was not amassed by millions or even thousands of federal workers. It was amassed by 435 House members, 100 senators and the president.

---

[7] Balance Due: Credit-Card Debt Nears $1 Trillion as Banks Push Plastic, www.wsj.com, 5/20/2016.

This is not really a fair assertion since there are no doubt a few good federal legislators who are trying to be responsible. Let's say that this debt was amassed by at least 218 House members, 51 senators and the president. In all, less than 300 people are culpable for burying the remaining 320 million of us under an inconceivable amount of debt.

The national debt is nearly $60,000 per citizen (which includes every man, woman and child). For most of us, our credit card debt is a fraction of this amount of debt particularly if it is divided among every man, woman and child in our family or respective household.

According to usdebtclock.org, over $6 trillion of our national debt is owed to foreign countries. Someday, these foreign countries (some of whom are not our allies) will want us to repay these loans in a currency that continues to hold significant value. What if someday, the U.S. dollar no longer has any value because for years we have printed money faster than we can create an equivalent amount of goods, value or wealth?

It begs the question: Why are these legislators in Washington and the president so committed to enslaving the rest of us? How much is enough?

Perhaps a better line of questioning is: When do we say enough? When do we take action?

Jeff Deist, the president of the Mises Institute, has made a compelling case that healthy societies build and invest for the future[8]. This standard is akin to the popular phrase of "paying it forward". Today, we are not paying it forward. Instead, we are obligating future generations to pay it backwards and we are doing so without their consent. In a time-traveling sense, these future citizens (e.g., our children and grandchildren) are suffering from a sophisticated form of taxation without representation. They rely on us to be responsible and we are failing them on a colossal basis. Our society today is certainly not healthy by the standard advanced by Mr. Deist and the only

---

[8] https://mises.org/library/free-lunch-over

remedy for those of us concerned about the future of our nation seems to be the hope that we pick the right candidates every two years.

Even if the best candidates are elected every two-years for the foreseeable future, this will not solve the long-term problems of this nation. At best, this will only assure us that after each election, things will not degrade as fast as they would have otherwise.

Today, we rely on electing the right politicians to represent our national, state and individual interests in the federal government. Many times, even with the "right" politicians elected, these representatives don't vote the way we think they should and they don't promote or advance our national interests to the media. It is all very frustrating.

It is frustrating because we are striving to overcome the systemic problems introduced by the 1913 Solution without ever addressing the actual issue. We can't fix systemic problems by electing individuals who are not committed to fixing the system. So far, very few are even acknowledging these issues are actual problems.

The degree to which we adhere to the Constitution determines our level of freedom. Our Constitution was designed to establish and protect our freedom as individuals. Part of this freedom allows us to create and operate businesses to aid our fellow man and to provide for our families. This freedom has allowed our nation to prosper like no other in history. Our history of prosperity is due to the knowledge, skills and ingenuity of entrepreneurs who have met the needs and wants of their customers in an environment of free markets and competition. The Constitution is the foundation of our national prosperity because it protects our individual freedom and (should) foster (or establish) a free market economy. It also confers specific (enumerated) power or authority to the federal government to protect us and our freedoms from external and even internal threats.

The federal government generally does not contribute directly to our prosperity, but is in essence, an overhead cost we must pay for a civil society. Through taxes, we pay for a justice system to adjudicate internal disputes and a military to protect our nation and our interests from external threats. While the various Constitutional functions of the federal government do not directly contribute to our prosperity, these functions are necessary and do contribute by establishing and sustaining the framework of our free market economy and our freedoms.

Today, many "public servants" and many within the media (and other special interests) are determined to undermine our Constitution and circumvent the limitations it imposes on the federal government. This cancerous movement within our nation must be stopped or our nation will not survive.

> *The system is broken.*
>
> *Continued reliance on electing the right people is folly.*

When those in the federal government make statements fostering civil unrest and divisiveness, it is likely to lead to violence between factions. A few within the federal government seem determined to compromise the authority of local police departments and erode public support for these law enforcement agencies. These federal public servants appear to be establishing the need for federal intervention. We already hear talk of new federal guidelines or regulations on policing. These new rules would transfer additional control to the federal government and grant additional power to those sowing these seeds of discontent. This follows a familiar pattern.

Since 1913, the federal government has fomented one crisis after another in one realm after another. When the crisis manifests, the federal government steps in to rescue us by expanding the scope and power of the federal government thereby sowing the seeds of the next crisis. Once this type of cycle is established within one industry, the instigators move to another industry or another aspect of our lives and repeat the process to initiate another cycle of crises.

As our federal government imposes more and more regulations, as it intentionally deviates from the provisions of our Constitution, we lose our freedom and our prospects for future prosperity. The federal government, the institution constituted to protect us, and our rights, may now pose a greater threat to our freedoms and our way of life than any other entity anywhere in the world.

Today, we see many elected officials and bureaucrats at all levels of government all too willing to sacrifice our freedom to increase their own power by re-interpreting the Constitution or by ignoring it all together. We can no longer rely on those in power to adhere to the Constitution and our nation is degrading faster and faster as a result. Rather than the democratic-republic established by our founding fathers, the lack of adherence to our Constitution means we will inevitably move closer and closer to a dictatorship or at the very least, an oligarchy.

The 17th Amendment opened the door to the abuse of power we see today. Only the closing of this door will re-establish the structure for a system of good governance. This may be our last chance to reclaim our heritage of individual freedom and re-establish our prospects for a bright future.

The problems of this nation are systemic and only a change to this system will fix these problems and improve our prospects for long-term prosperity. **Continued reliance on electing the right people is folly.** It is not a viable long-term strategy and it will assure us that our beloved nation will degrade to its ultimate demise.

Thankfully, only a few minor adjustments to our system are needed and we understand these adjustments. A repeal of the 17th Amendment is first and foremost. Since the ratification of the 17th Amendment, every duty, relationship and function of the Senate has been corrupted by special interests. The Senate no longer advances the interests of the several states or the nation at-large; the Senate can only be relied upon to advance the interests of the dominant political party. This does not bode well for our nation's future.

To summarize the reasons for a repeal of the 17th Amendment:

- The U.S. Senate is no longer fulfilling its Constitutional charter to faithfully represent the interests of the states or to advance the long-term interests of the nation
- The states no longer have a voice at the federal level
- The original separation of power has been compromised
- The division of power has also been compromised
- The Senate now advances special interests -- primarily those of the major political parties
- The new power structure established the framework for the federal leviathan
- The new power structure changed the legislative benchmark; new legislation does not have to be in the interests of a majority of states
- The new power structure also affects decisions regarding Senate confirmations (such as Supreme Court nominees, treaties with other nations and the declaration of war
- The Senate is no longer insulated from the media; instead, senators attempt to appease the mainstream media by conforming to their worldview

The remedy for many of the problems we see today is the restoration of the relationship of senators to their state legislatures.

Once the 16th Amendment is repealed and we have restored the Senate to a body faithfully representing the interests of the several states, we can have a serious and meaningful discussion regarding the 16th Amendment and the Federal Reserve. A complete elimination of the Federal Reserve System may not be warranted, but a complete review and audit of the Federal Reserve by the new Senate is warranted. Obviously we don't want to dismantle the Federal Reserve System unless we have a viable (and better) alternative.

As far as the 16th Amendment is concerned, many argue that the authorization to collect taxes from individuals is quite limited under the 16th. While this may be true, this certainly isn't the interpretation of the IRS and many within the federal government. Even if the 16th is limited in scope, there is obviously sufficient ambiguity to warrant its repeal in favor of a better system. The laws and policies of our government should be transparent, above board and consistent. The system we are currently coping with is ambiguous, misleading and convoluted and those within the IRS seem all too willing to exploit the situation to advance the cause of bigger and more intrusive government. Furthermore, we don't need tax revenue from individuals if we limited the federal government to the provisions specified in the Constitution.

Call to Action

If you agree with the repeal of the 17th Amendment, send a copy of this pamphlet to your state legislators, your family and friends. We need to generate a grassroots campaign to re-establish control over our nation. This is our last hope.

At the close of the Constitutional Convention in 1787, Benjamin Franklin was asked a question about the type of government created by the convention. He reportedly answered, "A republic, if you can keep it." This was a profound and prophetic statement. We are at an important point in our nation's history. The decision we make now (or our indecision) will either restore our nation or assure its eventual demise. The only way we are going to keep this republic is with the repeal of the 17th Amendment.

By December of 1913, the government had substantial new powers, a new source of revenue, unlimited credit and no adult supervision. A child's dream and soon, our representatives were acting very childlike starting an all too real nightmare for the rest of us. It is time to wake up, America. Let's wake up and fix the problems foisted on us by the 1913 Solution.

Afterword

Years ago, I took an oath to defend the Constitution against all enemies, foreign and domestic. I have dedicated much of my life to this cause to include supporting our brave men and women in uniform in various capacities. This pamphlet is the latest action I have taken to fulfill this oath.

On more than one occasion, I've mentioned to friends and family that if I complete a book on this subject, make a million dollars in sales and the 17th Amendment is not repeal, this endeavor has failed and I will be profoundly disappointed. If I don't make a dollar and the 17th Amendment is repealed, I will consider this to be an unmitigated success. I hope this relatively small gesture pays dividends to us all for many years to come.

Even more, I pray the efforts and sacrifices of our troops, our sailors and our airmen who have pledged their lives in defense of our Constitution have not been in vain. Right now, federal level elected officials and bureaucrats seem all too willing to compromise the sacrifices of these heroes by trampling the very Constitution these public servants have vowed to defend. This is a travesty in the truest sense.

Let's work together to keep this republic for the many who have sacrificed so much in its defense, their families and their descendants.